Find It in the
DESERT

Dee Phillips

GARETH**STEVENS**
PUBLISHING
A Member of the WRC Media Family of Companies

Please visit our web site at: **www.garethstevens.com**
For a free color catalog describing Gareth Stevens Publishing's list of high-quality books
and multimedia programs, call 1-800-542-2595 (USA) or 1-800-387-3178 (Canada).
Gareth Stevens Publishing's fax: (414) 332-3567.

Library of Congress Cataloging-in-Publication Data

Phillips, Dee, 1967-
    Find it in the desert / by Dee Phillips.
       p. cm. — (Can you find it?)
    ISBN 0-8368-6300-3 (lib. bdg.)
    1. Desert animals—Juvenile literature. 2. Desert plants—Juvenile literature. I. Title.
  QL116.P48 2006
  578.754—dc22
                                         2005056344

This North American edition first published in 2006 by
Gareth Stevens Publishing
A Member of the WRC Media Family of Companies
330 West Olive Street, Suite 100
Milwaukee, WI 53212 USA

This U.S. edition copyright © 2006 by Gareth Stevens, Inc. Original edition copyright © 2005 by
ticktock Entertainment Ltd. First published in Great Britain in 2005 by ticktock Media Ltd., Unit 2,
Orchard Business Centre, North Farm Road, Tunbridge Wells, Kent TN2 3XF.

Gareth Stevens series editor: Dorothy L. Gibbs
Gareth Stevens graphic designer: Charlie Dahl
Gareth Stevens art direction: Tammy West

Picture credits: (t=top, b=bottom, l=left, r=right, c=center)
Alamy: 4-5, 9. Ardea Images: 17. FLPA: 4-5, 6-7c, 10, 19.
Every effort has been made to trace the copyright holders for the pictures used in this book.
We apologize in advance for any unintentional omissions and would be pleased to insert the
appropriate acknowledgements in any subsequent edition.

Printed in the United States of America

1 2 3 4 5 6 7 8 9 10 09 08 07 06

Words that appear in the glossary are printed in
boldface type the first time they occur in the text.

Contents

The Desert

There is so much to see in the desert, from camels crossing the **parched** landscape to deadly snakes and scorpions.

What can you find in the desert?

Bighorn sheep

Joshua tree

Golden eagle

Cactus

Rattlesnake

Camel

Roadrunner

Gila monster

Desert tortoise

5

Bighorn Sheep

Bighorn sheep can be found today only in **remote** areas. All rams, which are male sheep, have big horns. The females, or ewes, have smaller horns.

A ram's horns can measure 30 inches (76 centimeters) around the curl.

When bighorn sheep have enough green plants to eat, they do not need to drink water.

Bighorn rams fight a lot, usually to show which ram is stronger.

In summer, bighorns rest during the day, when the weather is very hot.

Joshua Tree

Joshua trees are found in only one part of the world – the Mojave Desert in Arizona, Nevada, Utah and southwestern California.

The size of a Joshua tree can be anywhere from 15 to 40 feet (4.5 to 12 meters) tall.

A Joshua tree has sword-shaped **evergreen** leaves and clusters of small, creamy white flowers.

People say this tree was named after the **prophet** Joshua in the Bible, who waved his arms in the air to point the way to the **promised land.**

Golden Eagle

The golden eagle is one of the largest birds of prey in the world. It gets its name from the golden feathers on its head.

The broad wings of a golden eagle are ideal for soaring high over mountains.

A golden eagle has a razor-sharp beak that can easily tear the flesh of its **prey**.

The golden eagle's powerful *talons*, hooked beak, and sharp eyesight all combine to make this bird a deadly **predator**.

11

Cactus

There are many different types of cactus plants. All types are able to live in deserts because they can go without water for a long time.

Birds such as wrens and woodpeckers often nest in cactus plants.

Most cacti have needlelike spines that help protect the plants from being eaten by animals.

The inside of a cactus stem is spongy or **hollow**, which helps the plant hold and store water.

13

Rattlesnake

Rattlesnakes are **venomous** reptiles found only in North America. Because they are often captured or killed by hunters, these large snakes are becoming **rare**.

The rattlesnake gets its name from the rattling sound it makes when it shakes its tail.

Like all snakes, a rattlesnake uses its tongue to smell the air.

The largest rattlesnake is the Eastern Diamondback. It can grow to almost 8 feet (2.5 m) long.

Camel

A camel has either one or two humps, which it uses to store fat. The fat a camel stores helps keep the animal alive during long journeys across the desert.

Camels have hooved feet with thick pads on the bottoms. A camel's wide feet keep it from sinking into the soft desert sand.

Bactrian camels have two humps. They live in the deserts of central Asia. Camels that have only one hump live in Arab countries. They are called dromedaries.

Roadrunner

A roadrunner is a large bird with brown-and-white striped feathers.

Roadrunners live in the deserts of the western United States and Mexico.

A roadrunner has long, thin legs. It also has long tail feathers, which it carries high in the air.

On the top of its head, a roadrunner has a spiky crest of feathers.

Roadrunners can fly, but they usually either walk or run. They can run fast enough to catch rattlesnakes, which are among their favorite foods.

19

Gila Monster

A gila monster is a poisonous lizard with pink-and-black skin. It lives in the deserts of North America.

Gila monsters have long tongues – and **fangs!**

Lizards are **cold-blooded** animals. They **bask** in the Sun to stay warm, and they cool down in the shade.

Tough, scaly skin helps protect a gila monster when it is attacked by a predator.

Desert Tortoise

This tortoise spends most of its life under the soft sand of the desert. The sand protects it from the hot sun and freezing cold nights.

A hard shell called a carapace covers the soft body of a desert tortoise.

When the tortoise senses danger, it pulls its head, legs, and tail all the way inside its shell.

A desert tortoise eats grass, herbs, and other plants and can live for up to eighty years.

Glossary

bask – to lie in the warmth of the Sun

birds of prey – meat-eating birds, such as eagles and hawks, that hunt and kill small mammals for food

cold-blooded – having a body that does not make its own heat and is heated or cooled by its surroundings

evergreen – staying alive and green all year round

fangs – hollow, pointed teeth used for biting and injecting poison

hollow – empty inside

parched – extremely dry

predator – an animal that hunts and kills other animals for food

prey – an animal that is killed by another animal for food

promised land – a term used to mean heaven, or a place of peace where life goes on after death

prophet – a deeply spiritual person who is guided by God or a higher power to foretell future events

rare – uncommon or hard to find

remote – far away from towns and cities

talons – long, sharp claws used for grabbing and holding prey as well as for tearing it apart

venomous – containing venom, or poison